BOOK OF FLIGHT

10 Record-Breaking Animals with Wings

by Gabrielle Balkan
illustrated by Sam Brewster

To the good people at 500womenscientists.org – GSB

For all the adults who are still asking "why?" - SB

Thank you for the know-how and generosity of animal experts Allyson Coleman, Animal Curator at Leesburg Animal Park in Leesburg, Virginia; Anthony Friscia, Ph.D., Professor of Integrative Biology & Physiology at UCLA, Los Angeles, California; Lee "Boneman" Post, an animal bone enthusiast in Homer, Alaska; Dr. Maggie Watson, a seabird researcher and lecturer at Charles Sturt University in Albury, Australia; and the library staff at the Natural History Museum, London. I would not be nearly as informed or pleased without you!

Phaidon Press Inc.
65 Bleecker Street
New York, NY 10012

phaidon.com

First published 2019
© 2019 Phaidon Press Limited
Text copyright © Gabrielle Balkan
Illustration copyright © Sam Brewster

Artwork created with ink on paper and digital coloring
Typeset in Raisonné and Value Serif

ISBN 978 0 7148 7863 8 (US edition)
002-0319

Designed by Meagan Bennett

Printed in China

3 9547 00448 7554

TABLE OF CONTENTS

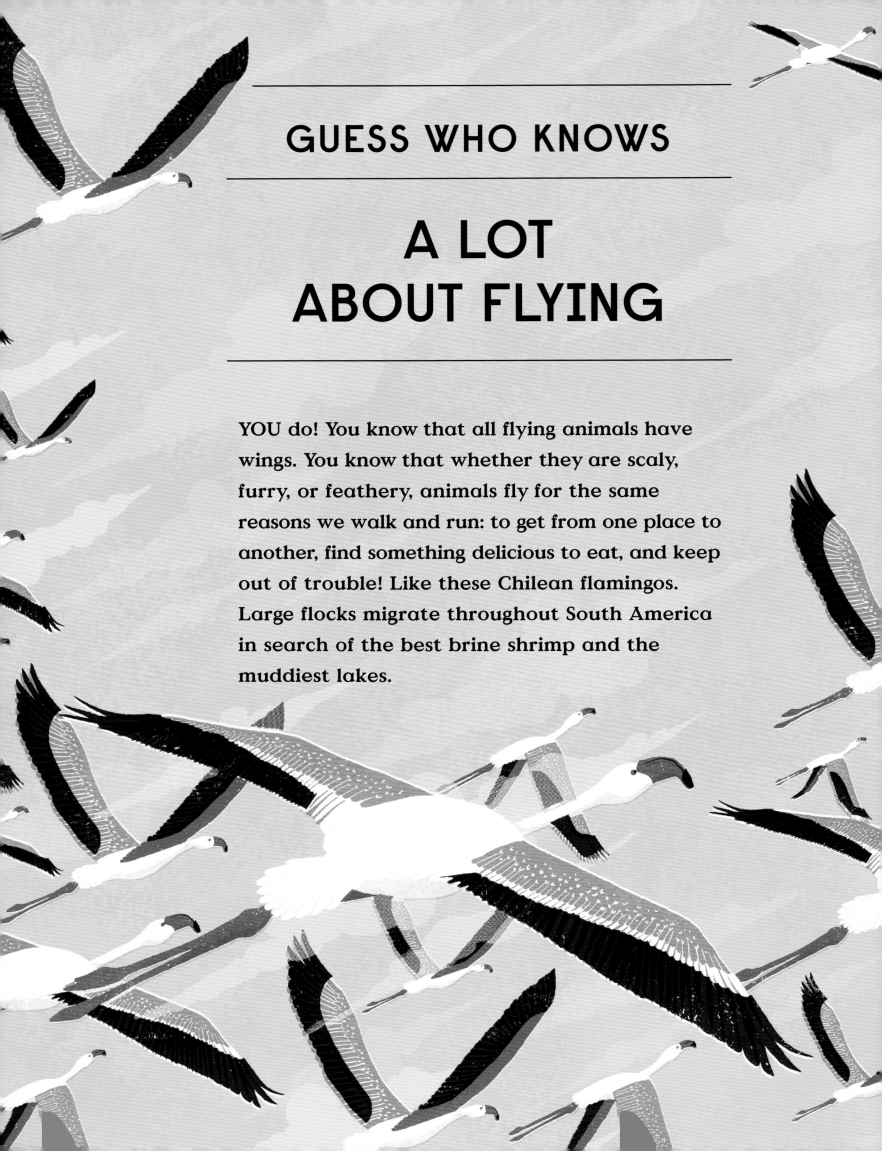

GUESS WHO KNOWS

A LOT ABOUT FLYING

YOU do! You know that all flying animals have wings. You know that whether they are scaly, furry, or feathery, animals fly for the same reasons we walk and run: to get from one place to another, find something delicious to eat, and keep out of trouble! Like these Chilean flamingos. Large flocks migrate throughout South America in search of the best brine shrimp and the muddiest lakes.

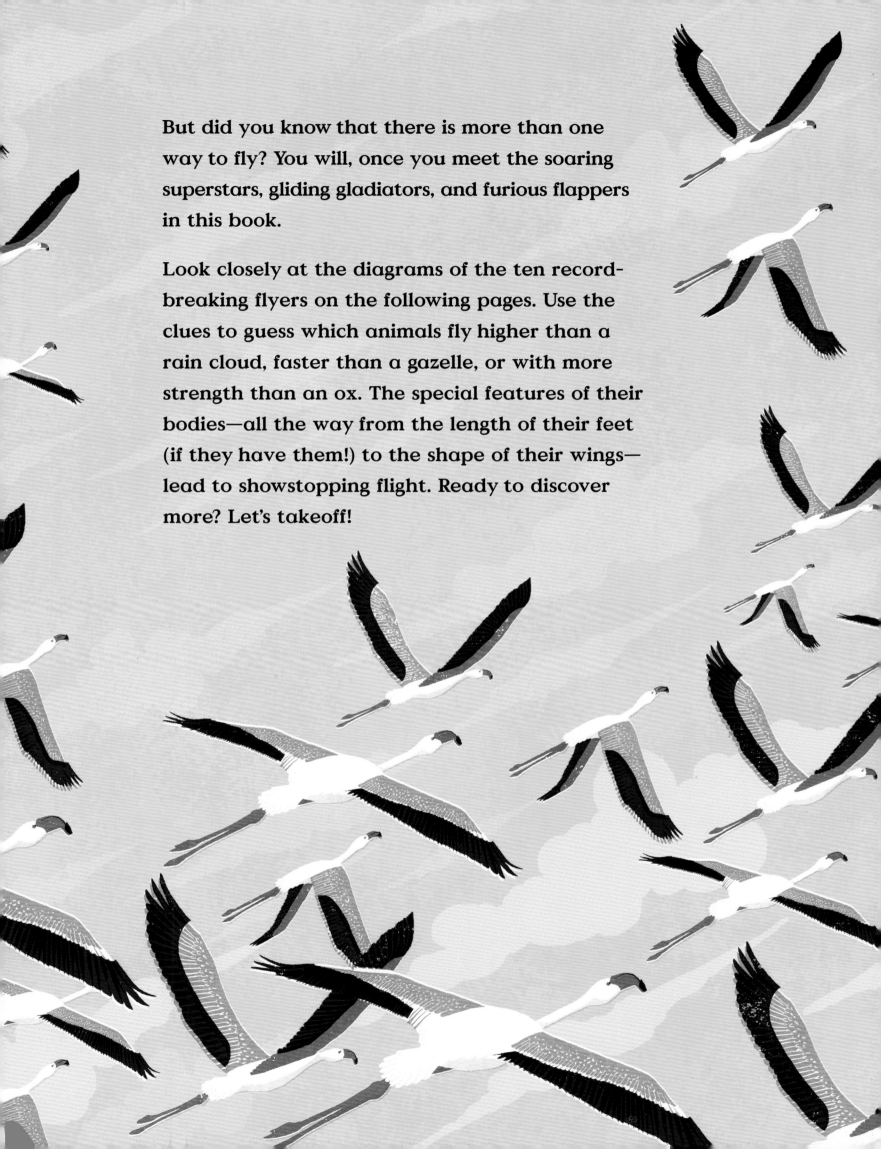

But did you know that there is more than one way to fly? You will, once you meet the soaring superstars, gliding gladiators, and furious flappers in this book.

Look closely at the diagrams of the ten record-breaking flyers on the following pages. Use the clues to guess which animals fly higher than a rain cloud, faster than a gazelle, or with more strength than an ox. The special features of their bodies—all the way from the length of their feet (if they have them!) to the shape of their wings—lead to showstopping flight. Ready to discover more? Let's takeoff!

GUESS WHO IS

THE FASTEST FLYER

Greyhound dogs and Olympic skiers break oodles of speed records. But I'm faster. I dash through Australian skies at a zesty 105 miles per hour. No other bird can do this. Falcons break speed records while diving. But I break records while soaring straight ahead. I flap with brisk up-and-down wingbeats to streak past clouds. I move my oversized wings close to my sides to make lightning-fast changes in direction. *Zoom!*

- Every summer, I migrate to lay a clutch of two eggs in Asia.

- I swallow flying ants and bees for breakfast. *Yum!*

- I'm named for the needlelike tips of my tail feathers.

My 20 inch wingspan is about the width of these two pages.

I am nearly 8 inches long, the length of a large banana.

High-speed wings like mine are long, thin, and end in a point.

Tiny feet and short legs make me weigh less, which makes me fly faster. My feet are so small and difficult to see that people once thought I didn't have any.

This stubby tail is no good as a rudder, so I steer with my wings.

My skeleton is made of narrow, hollow bones: evolution's way of making me light enough to fly.

Who am I?

I AM A
WHITE-THROATED
NEEDLETAIL

My extra long, extra rigid wings make me the fastest cruiser. To get to where we need to go and to eat what we need to eat, we swifts spend 10 months out of every year in the air. That's more than any other bird.

I do just about everything while I fly, even sleep. To snooze, I first climb two miles above the earth. Then I slowly drift down for a 30-minute power nap.

When I stop to nest, I must land someplace high, like a tree hollow. I can't take off from the ground with my combination of short legs and long wings. When it's time to fly, I drop straight down and plunge nine feet. It's only when there's room for my wings to move that I can swoop up and regain my place as the fastest flyer in the world.

GUESS WHO IS

THE MOST UNPREDICTABLE FLYER

You'll never guess where I'm going. That's my plan. Compared to the birds that want to eat me, I'm weak and seemingly defenseless. I don't have claws or a beak for protection. Plus, I weigh less than a tea bag! You could stomp me into oblivion. But first, you'd have to catch me. Fluttering around with quick zigs and zags gives me my best chance at survival. This strategy makes it impossible for predators to predict which way I'll fly. I'm safe!

- I lay eggs on the underside of leaves in the high mountains of India.

- For my first meal, I munch my own eggshell. *Tasty!*

- My four wings tear easily and I can't repair them.

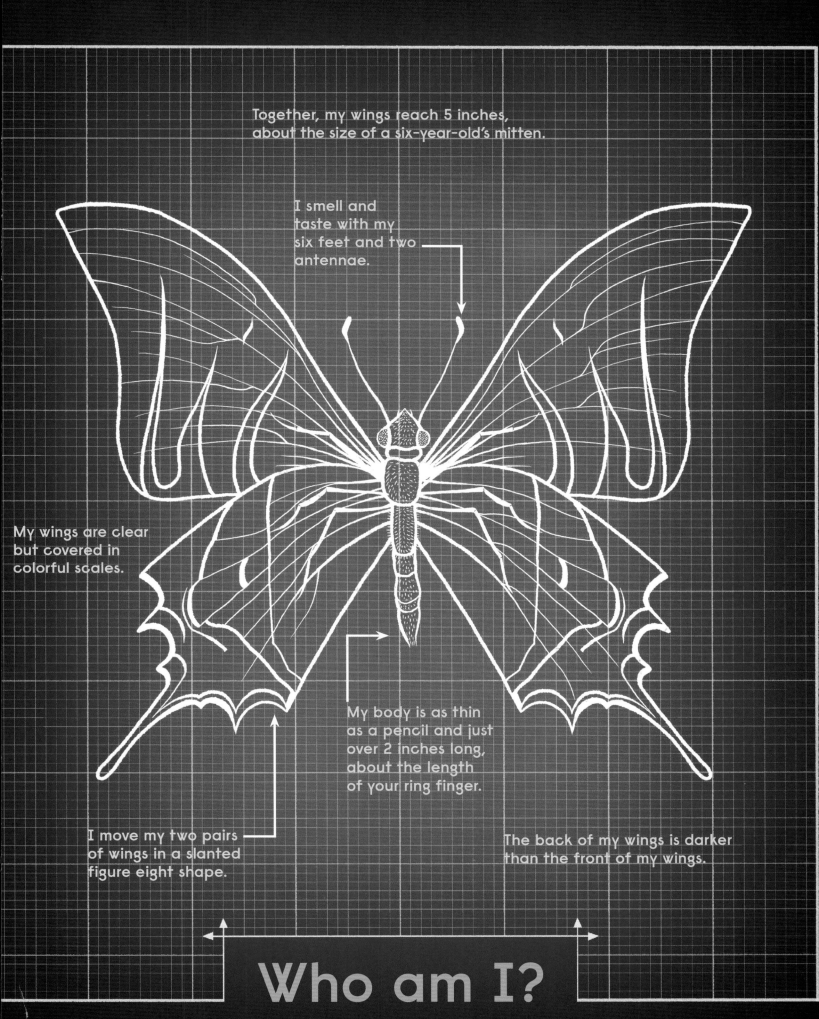

I AM A
KAISER-I-HIND
BUTTERFLY

My name means "Emperor of India" in Hindi. All butterflies are unpredictable flyers, but I am one of the planet's rarest swallowtails, celebrated for the stunning colors on the underside of my wings.

My wings are covered in tiny, brightly colored scales, arranged like shingles on a roof. These scales provide strength and a place for air to collect. This combo gives me a boost and lets me fly higher.

Like all butterflies, I'm famous for abrupt changes in direction. The massive size of a butterfly's wing is what makes us unpredictable flyers. They act like the rudder of a ship. The bigger the rudder, the faster the turn. The flight of a butterfly looks a bit like a game of tag: we duck and weave, just like you might to avoid being caught. Care to join me in a game? You're it!

GUESS WHO IS

THE BEST FLYING ACROBAT

Scoop, tuck, tumble, flip! The secret to my acrobatic flight lies in the many bones and joints of my wings. They're built just like your hands, but my fingers are much longer—and webbed! I pull my fingers together to change the shape of my wings. Then I push air behind me to swoop and dive with more precision than any other animal. I zip along at 38 miles an hour, then dart into the nook of a tree, flip over, and hang upside down by my toes.

- I sleep during the day in the treetops of Madagascar.

- I eat lychees, mangoes, and other fruit. *Delish!*

- No feathers here—my wings are made from thin, smooth skin.

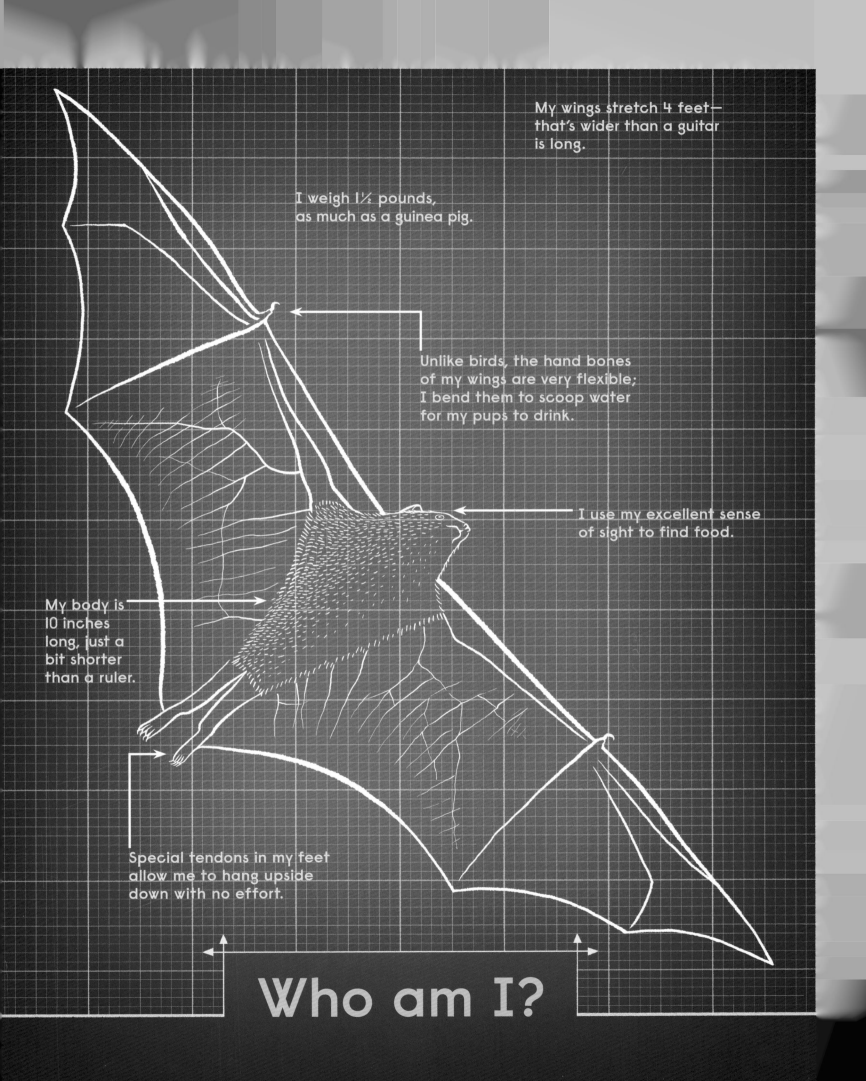

My wings stretch 4 feet—
that's wider than a guitar
is long.

I weigh 1½ pounds,
as much as a guinea pig.

Unlike birds, the hand bones
of my wings are very flexible;
I bend them to scoop water
for my pups to drink.

I use my excellent sense
of sight to find food.

My body is
10 inches
long, just a
bit shorter
than a ruler.

Special tendons in my feet
allow me to hang upside
down with no effort.

Who am I?

I AM A MADAGASCAN FLYING FOX

I'm named for my furry face and fox-like snout. I'm a megabat, the largest type of bat. Like all bats, my wings are HEAVY. They're filled with muscles that give us maximum control over our bendy wings. This strength and flexibility makes us bats the best flying acrobats.

I spend my days roosting with 400 others in a noisy bat colony. At night, I take my gymnastics to the sky, sometimes flying 20 miles in search of a meal.

Smaller microbats use echolocation to find insects to eat. We megabats use our excellent sense of sight and smell to find food. I can eat up to my own weight in figs and other fruit. If you ate your weight in food, you'd eat more than 100 bananas before bed!

GUESS WHO IS

THE STRONGEST FLYER

I'm stronger than you. Don't argue, I can explain: I can carry animals more than twice my size. I've even been known to carry a small pig. That's like you lifting a baby rhino. I use my long legs and powerful feet to grab hold of my prey and stop it from fighting back. Then I use my strong chest muscles to flap my mighty wings and fly dinner back to my nest. I have zero point zero predators— I'm that intimidating!

- I build an enormous nest in the trees of the Philippines.

- I eat snakes, colugos, and macaque monkeys. *Burp.*

- I lay a single egg just once every two years or so.

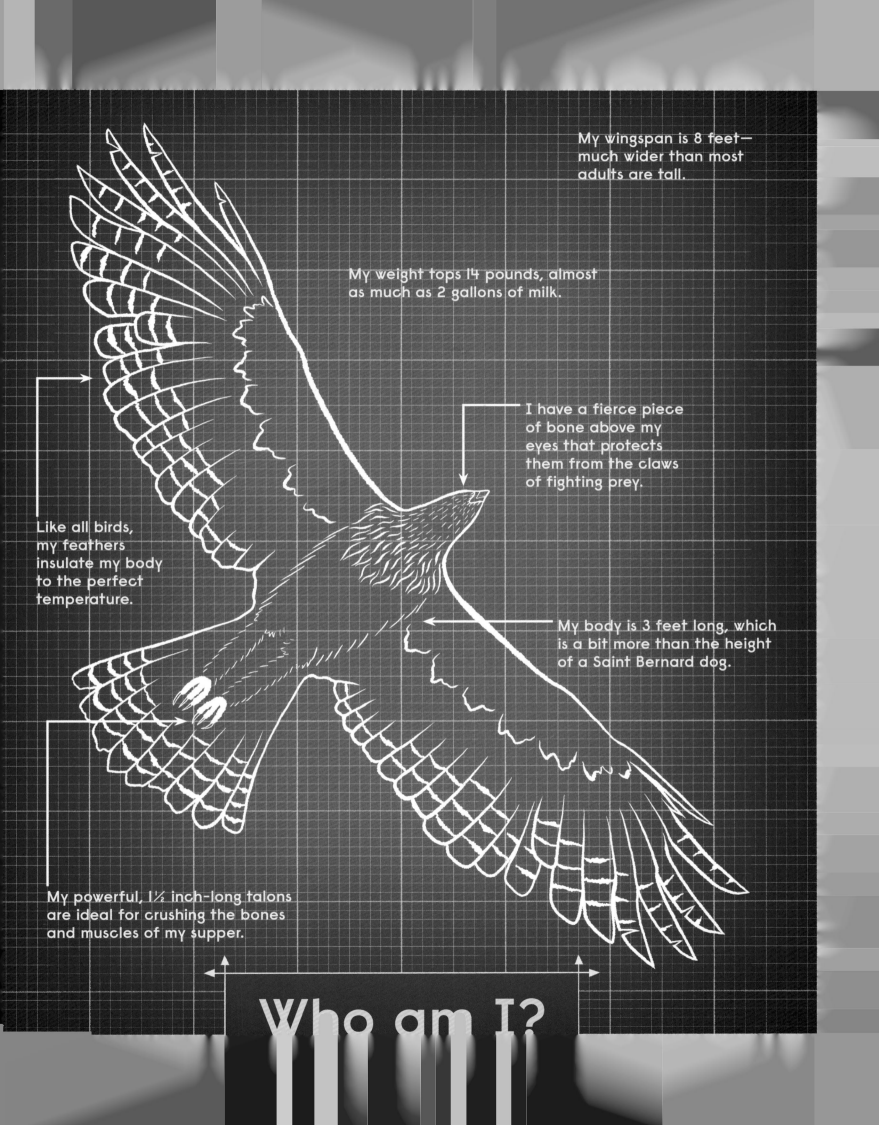

My wingspan is 8 feet—much wider than most adults are tall.

My weight tops 14 pounds, almost as much as 2 gallons of milk.

I have a fierce piece of bone above my eyes that protects them from the claws of fighting prey.

Like all birds, my feathers insulate my body to the perfect temperature.

My body is 3 feet long, which is a bit more than the height of a Saint Bernard dog.

My powerful, 1½ inch-long talons are ideal for crushing the bones and muscles of my supper.

Who am I?

I AM A PHILIPPINE EAGLE

All eagles are strong but I am also the world's largest and rarest eagle. Like all tough birds of prey, I have a sharp, hooked beak—perfect for tearing flesh from my meal. I can even tear the tail from a monkey.

My hunt begins with my powerful eyes: seeing possible eats in full detail from a great distance. Even my vision is eight times as sharp as yours! Then, I hone in, spreading my broad wings for a slow flight above the dense forest. Like most birds, I lower my tail feathers to steer downward and get closer to my prey.

Once I have my edible prize, I master the hardest part of flying—taking off from the ground. I use my big chest muscles to hit the sky. Doing this is like you trying to jump a hurdle without a running start *and* while carrying a friend! Powerful stuff, right?

GUESS WHO IS

THE BEST AT HOVERING

I am the helicopter of the insect world. Most animals that fly need to move *forward* to have lift. But I can hang suspended in space, flapping my wings 30 times a second to stay in one spot. Birds flap their wings in unison—at the same time and in the same direction. I, however, flap each of my four wings in four different directions at the exact same time. This gives me complete control to fly any way I like: backward, sideways, upside down, and to even hover in the same place.

- I hover over freshwater ponds in Africa and Europe.

- I snatch gnats and mayflies, devouring them in flight. *Chomp!*

- I spend most of my life as a nymph (a baby insect), swimming in the water.

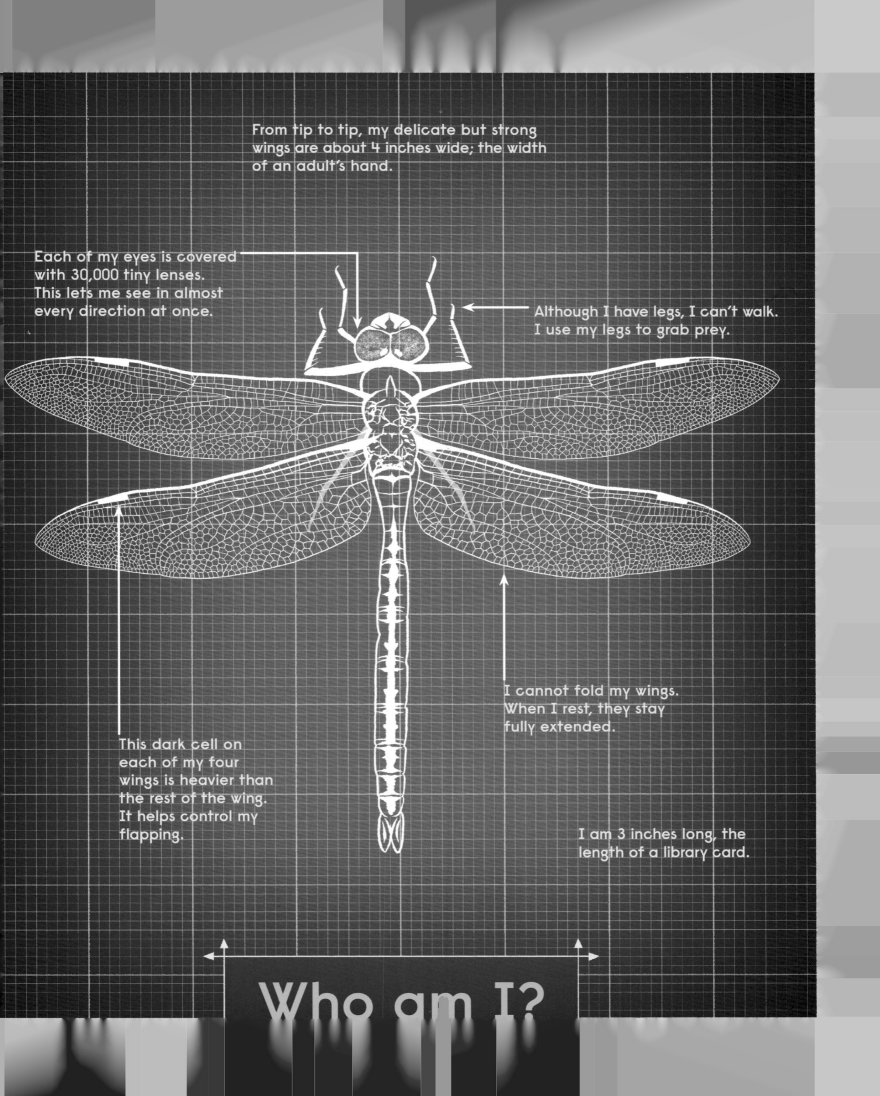

From tip to tip, my delicate but strong wings are about 4 inches wide; the width of an adult's hand.

Each of my eyes is covered with 30,000 tiny lenses. This lets me see in almost every direction at once.

Although I have legs, I can't walk. I use my legs to grab prey.

This dark cell on each of my four wings is heavier than the rest of the wing. It helps control my flapping.

I cannot fold my wings. When I rest, they stay fully extended.

I am 3 inches long, the length of a library card.

Who am I?

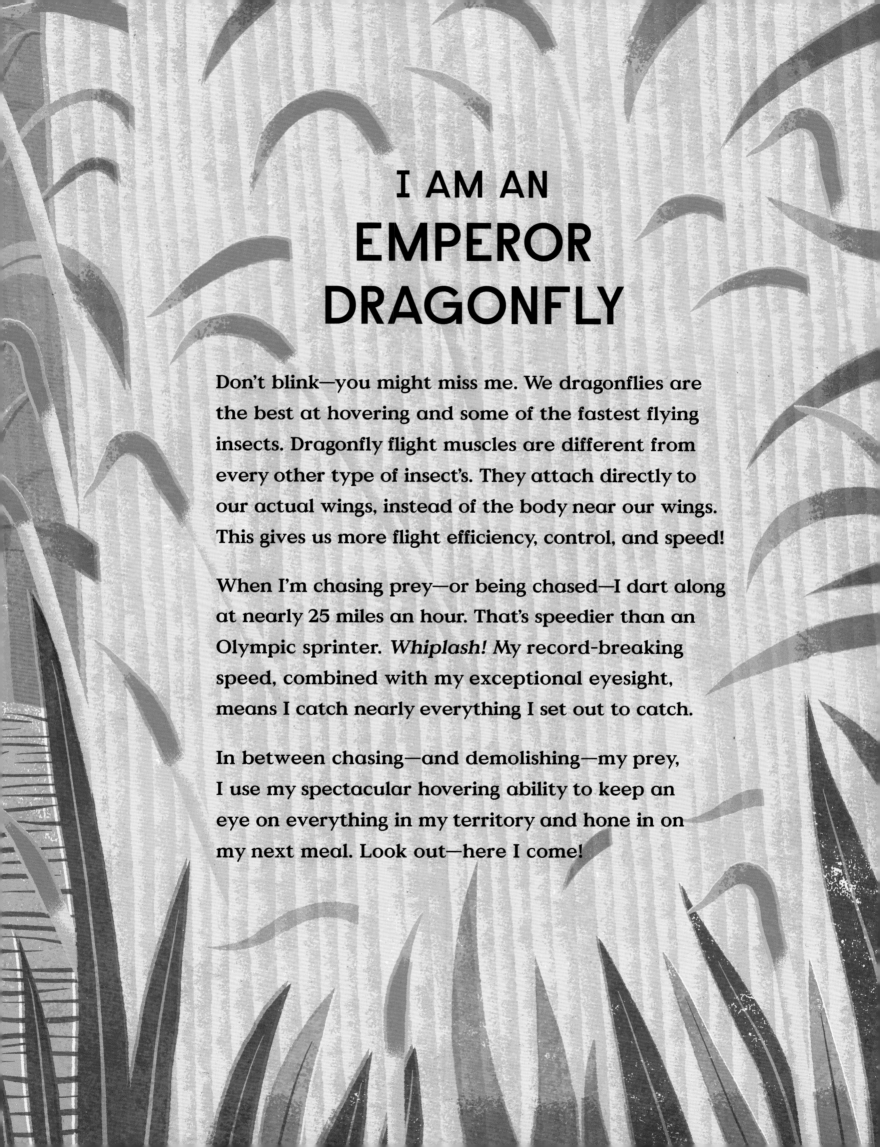

I AM AN EMPEROR DRAGONFLY

Don't blink—you might miss me. We dragonflies are the best at hovering and some of the fastest flying insects. Dragonfly flight muscles are different from every other type of insect's. They attach directly to our actual wings, instead of the body near our wings. This gives us more flight efficiency, control, and speed!

When I'm chasing prey—or being chased—I dart along at nearly 25 miles an hour. That's speedier than an Olympic sprinter. *Whiplash!* My record-breaking speed, combined with my exceptional eyesight, means I catch nearly everything I set out to catch.

In between chasing—and demolishing—my prey, I use my spectacular hovering ability to keep an eye on everything in my territory and hone in on my next meal. Look out—here I come!

THE BEST
AT GLIDING

It's a bird, it's a plane! Aaaactually, it's neither; it's me, a beautiful brown reptile, hurtling 30 feet from tree to tree. My wings aren't feathered like a bird, or scaled like a butterfly. Instead, each wing is a patagium: a smooth flap of skin. Other gliding animals, like some bats, squirrels, and colugos have patagia, too. But mine are attached to my ribs, which I can open and close, like a living fan. I open my patagia when I leap from a tall tree and then glide to another, sometimes traveling as far as 100 feet away.

- I live in the thick forests of southern India.

- Ants and termites make up my breakfast. And lunch. And dinner.

- I am a cold-blooded, four-legged reptile.

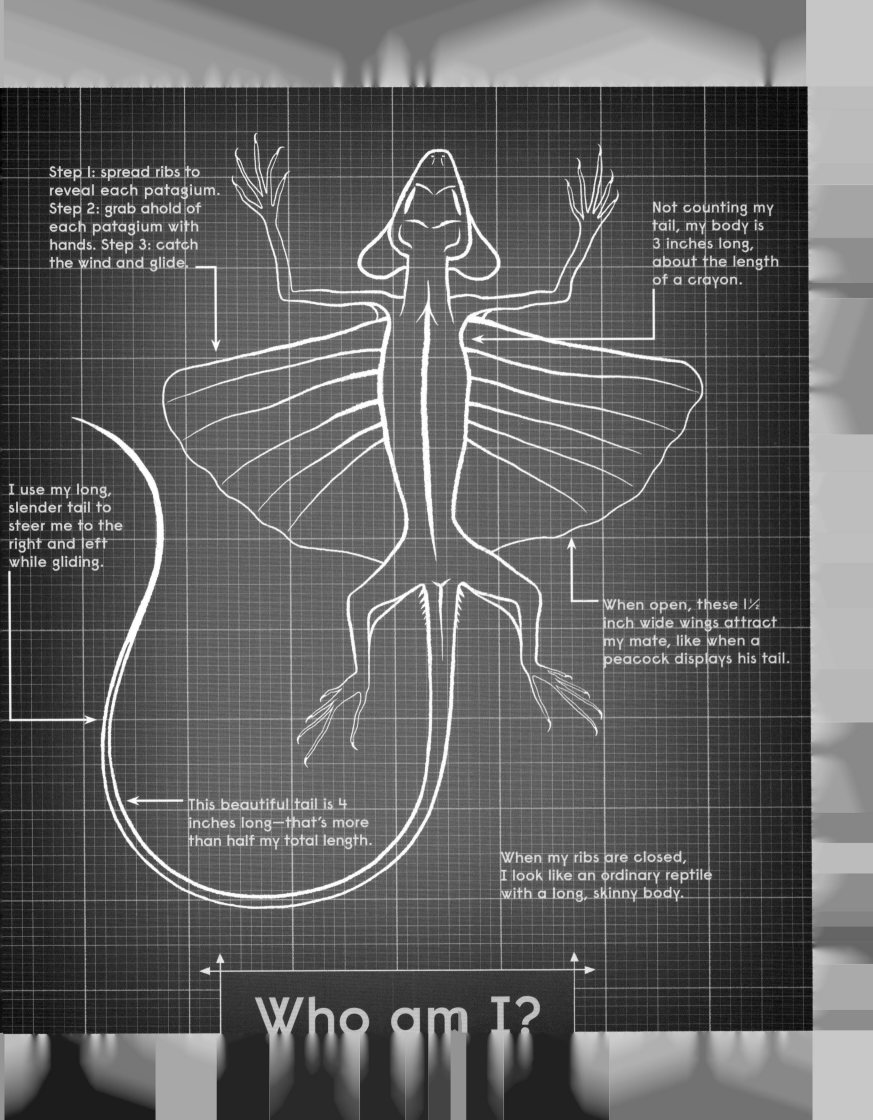

Step 1: spread ribs to reveal each patagium. Step 2: grab ahold of each patagium with hands. Step 3: catch the wind and glide.

Not counting my tail, my body is 3 inches long, about the length of a crayon.

I use my long, slender tail to steer me to the right and left while gliding.

When open, these 1½ inch wide wings attract my mate, like when a peacock displays his tail.

This beautiful tail is 4 inches long—that's more than half my total length.

When my ribs are closed, I look like an ordinary reptile with a long, skinny body.

Who am I?

I AM A
DRAGO LIZARD

I'm often called a flying dragon. I don't breathe fire but I will flare my dewlap—a flap of skin under my chin—at anyone who dares to move into my tree.

With lots of predators on the prowl, it's dangerous for me on the ground. Instead I live in the top layers of the forest's canopy. I spend my day racing up and down 400-foot-tall tree trunks. To find food and chase—or get away from—a challenge, I glide to another tree. That's like jumping and gliding between the 40th floors of skyscrapers!

The only time you'll see one of us gliding lizards on the ground is when a female lays eggs. Even then, her stay is short: a mere 24 hours of guarding the eggs and then she returns to the trees. Good luck, eggies! You'll need it.

GUESS WHO IS

THE BEST AT FLYING BACKWARD

Buzz, zip, hummmm! That's the sound of my wings moving at breakneck speed, taking me from flower to flower. My wings can beat up to 80 times a second—too fast for you to see. They are unlike the wings of any other bird. I swivel my wings nearly 180 degrees at the shoulder to make tiny figure eights. Something like a symphony conductor gracefully moving their wrists. This lets me whip the air and get lift with each up-and-down stroke—instead of just the downstroke. The result? I can hover, move forward, side to side, upside down, and yes, backward.

- I flicker through the warm mountains of South America.

- I sip nectar from deep cups of the fragrant passion flower. *Glug, glug.*

- I hatch from an egg the size of a jelly bean.

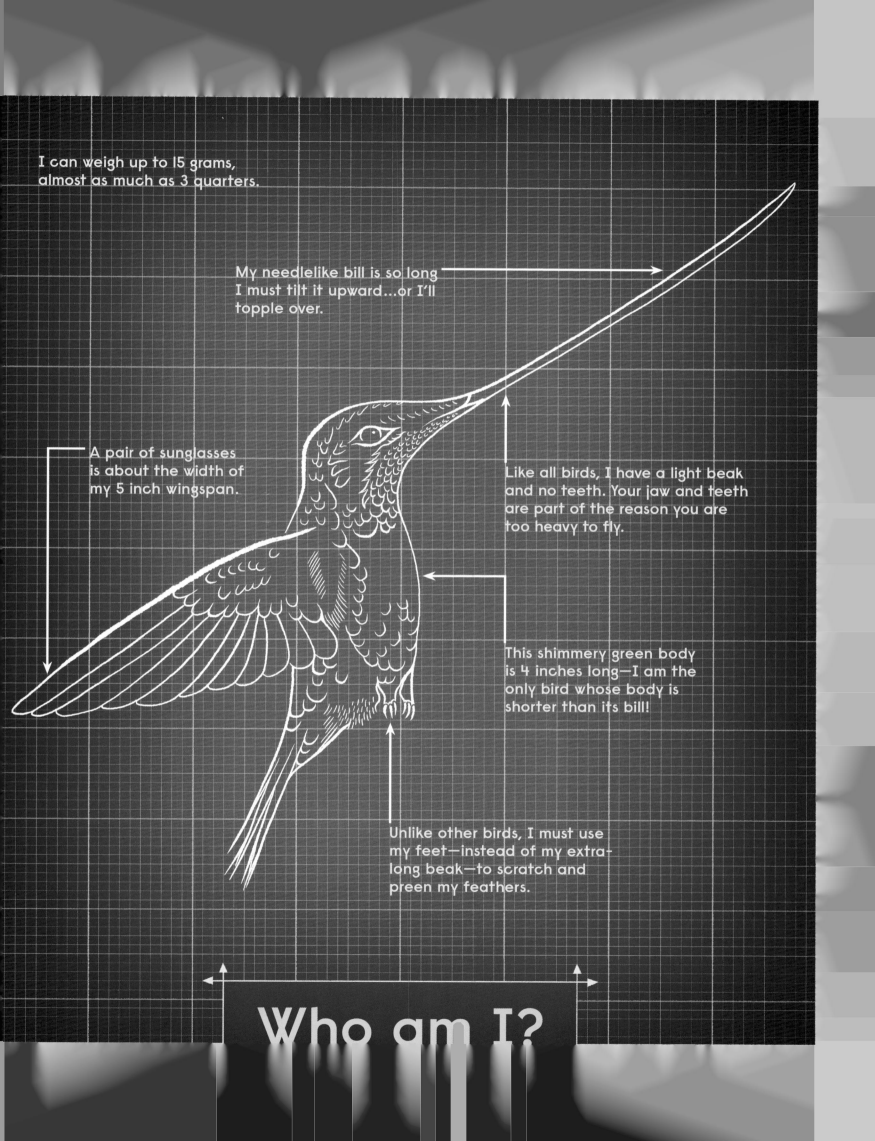

I can weigh up to 15 grams, almost as much as 3 quarters.

My needlelike bill is so long I must tilt it upward…or I'll topple over.

A pair of sunglasses is about the width of my 5 inch wingspan.

Like all birds, I have a light beak and no teeth. Your jaw and teeth are part of the reason you are too heavy to fly.

This shimmery green body is 4 inches long—I am the only bird whose body is shorter than its bill!

Unlike other birds, I must use my feet—instead of my extra-long beak—to scratch and preen my feathers.

Who am I?

I AM A
SWORD-BILLED
HUMMINGBIRD

Not only are we hummingbirds the best at flying backward, we are the ONLY birds that can.

Aside from looking pretty, being able to fly backward allows us to enjoy a meal that no other bird can get to: plant nectar! To sup, I unfurl my long, straw-like tongue to lick nectar 13 times a second—all while flying!

I spend most of my time on the go, flying forward and backward to visit over 1,000 flowers in one day. During this time, I eat every 10 minutes, and drink up to three times my body weight in sweet nectar. That's like *you* drinking 100 glasses of orange juice at breakfast, lunch, and dinner—*slurp!*

GUESS WHO IS

THE BEST
AT PARACHUTING

From adorable snout to sweet tail, I am covered in thick, snuggly fur. Under this fur I have a surprising feature. When I spread my arms and legs I expose my giant patagium, a strong, cape-like flap of skin. This skin lets me fly from tall tree to tall tree—without a single feather. Once I leap, my patagium catches the air—just like a parachute—and delivers me to safety, up to 100 yards away—about the length of a soccer field.

- I hide in the tropical rainforests of Southeast Asia.

- I chew on the soft parts of fruits and young leaves. *Munch, munch.*

- I use my patagium like a sling to carry my young.

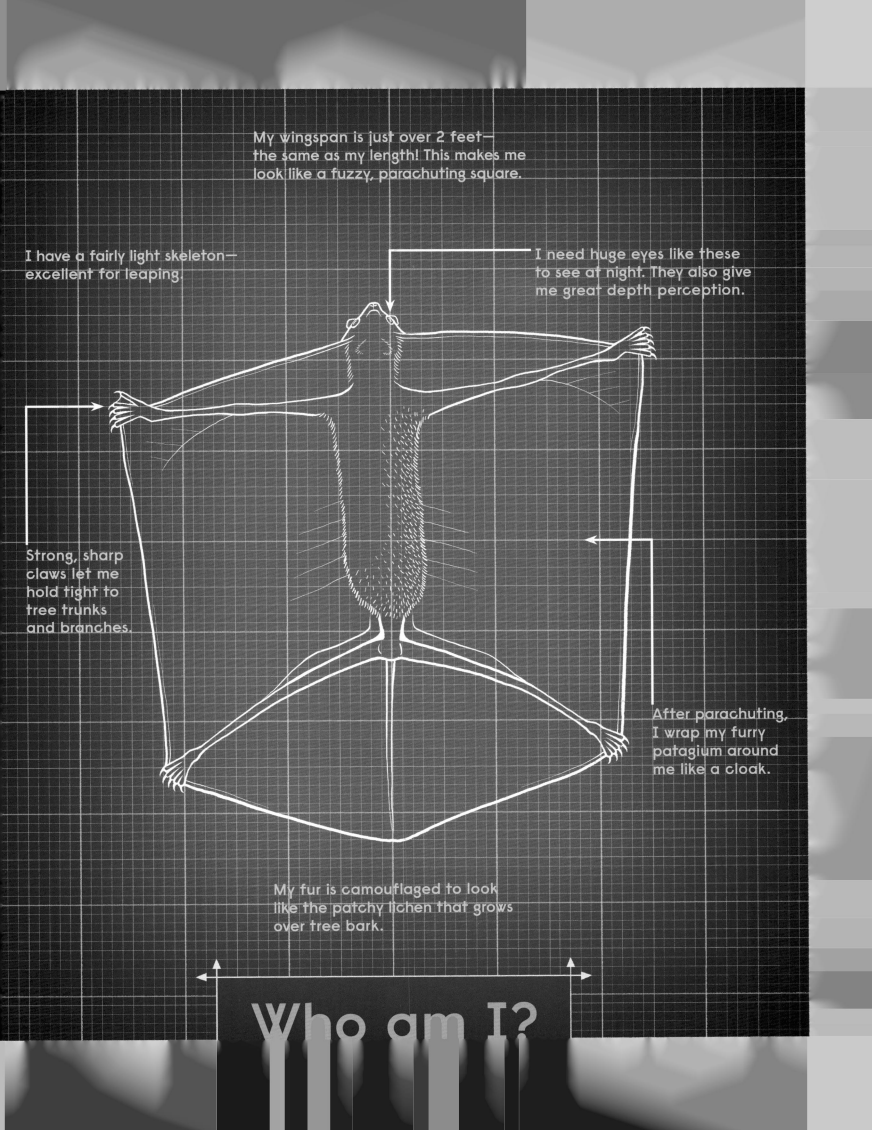

My wingspan is just over 2 feet—
the same as my length! This makes me
look like a fuzzy, parachuting square.

I have a fairly light skeleton—
excellent for leaping.

I need huge eyes like these
to see at night. They also give
me great depth perception.

Strong, sharp
claws let me
hold tight to
tree trunks
and branches.

After parachuting,
I wrap my furry
patagium around
me like a cloak.

My fur is camouflaged to look
like the patchy lichen that grows
over tree bark.

Who am I?

I AM A
MALAYAN
COLUGO

I spend my entire life parachuting around the same handful of trees. My kitelike patagium helps me do this quickly—and safely—so that I can find food.

I sleep all day, and at night spring into action to show off my unique ability. I sometimes travel up to two miles a night in search of just the right plants. Traveling by ground would take too long. Plus, while my extra skin makes for a beautiful parachute in the sky, it makes me quite helpless on the earth. It's like trying to crawl with a quilt attached to your hands and feet.

Instead of making my cumbersome way down a tree, across the ground, and up again, I leap, glide, then parachute to safety against the bark of a neighboring tree.

GUESS WHO IS

THE HIGHEST FLYER

Don't try to follow me—you'll die. I am the only bird that can soar as high as an airplane. Here, five miles above the earth, the air is too thin for you to breathe. My special blood type lets me survive and soar for hours, looking for something tasty to eat. But first I wait for the sun to heat my rocky perch. Then I capture the warm air currents in my giant wings and rise, something like a feathered hot air balloon.

- I lay a single egg on the rocky cliffs of central Africa.

- I sometimes climb into the ribcage of a dead animal to eat its flesh. *Dig in!*

- Unlike other birds of prey, I don't need to catch my dinner—just find it.

At 8 feet wide, my wingspan is the length of a motorcycle.

I am bald. This helps keep me from overheating. It's just a bonus that it is easier to clean blood off smooth skin than off feathers.

My sense of smell...stinks. I find all food by sight.

I'm 3 feet long, the height of a toddler.

This impressive bill has a slight hook, perfect for tearing flesh and crunching bone.

The acids in my gut let me digest rotting meat that would kill all other animals—including you.

Who am I?

I AM A
RÜPPELL'S GRIFFON VULTURE

There are 23 species of vultures and I am one of the largest. My huge wingspan lets me reach fast-flowing air currents found 30,000 feet up. Once I hitch a ride on a jet stream I am able to cover a massive distance with very little effort. In fact, I flap my wings only about once a minute.

I leave the sky when I spot dinner. Carrion. You know what that means? I eat dead animals. Wildebeest, antelope, zebra…it's all good, as long as it's dead.

I can eat about 20 percent of my body weight in one sitting. I sometimes eat so much that I can't fly. Then, I have to hobble to a tree and wait for the next day's warm air currents to give me a lift.

THE LOWEST FLYER

Ring-a-ling-ling! That dinner bell means it's time to fly. I fly, not to eat, but to avoid being eaten. It's not easy to hide in my home in the wide-open ocean. Whenever a big fish like a tuna threatens me, I leave my natural habitat and take to the air. Underwater, I flick my powerful tail from side to side to propel myself forward. Once I reach 35 miles per hour, I leap from the water, hold my breath, and glide for 30 seconds at a time.

- Find me in the warm waters off the coast of California.

- At night, I close in on the surface of the water to sample itty-bity plankton. *Chow time.*

- I lay thousands of eggs on drifting patches of kelp beds.

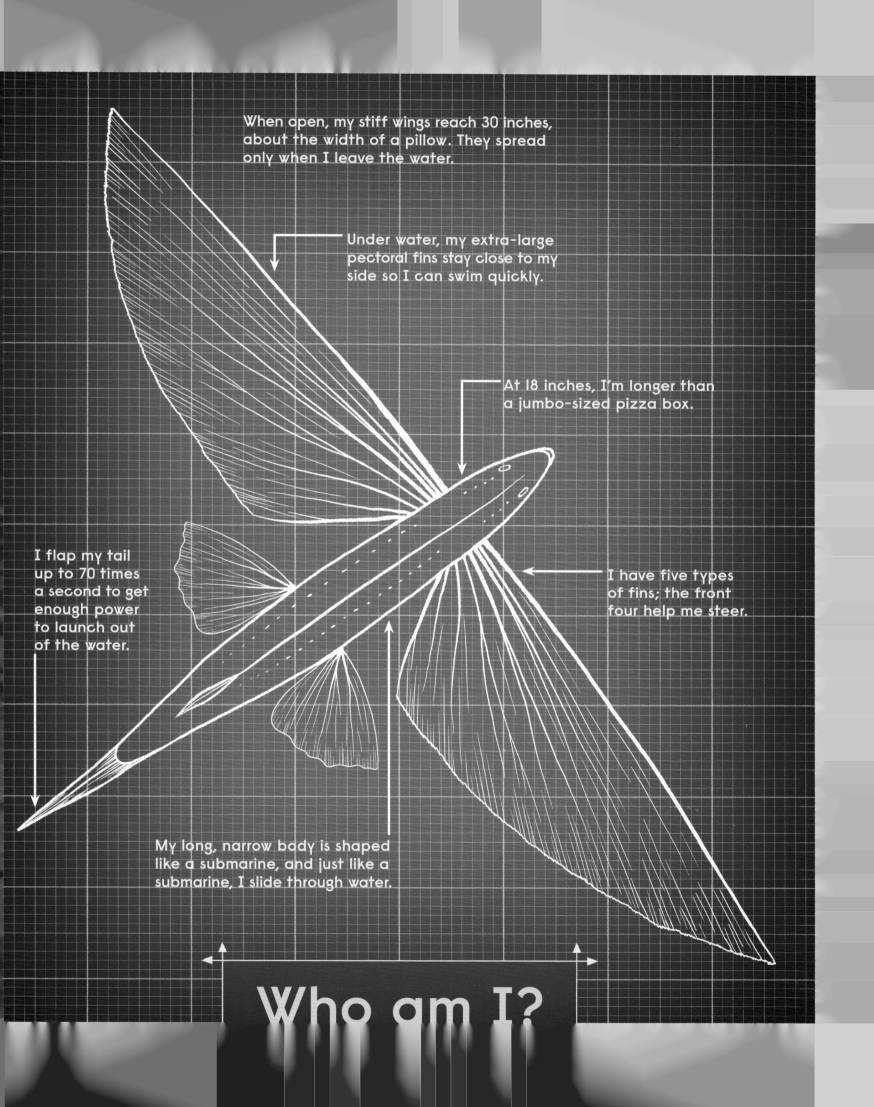

When open, my stiff wings reach 30 inches, about the width of a pillow. They spread only when I leave the water.

Under water, my extra-large pectoral fins stay close to my side so I can swim quickly.

At 18 inches, I'm longer than a jumbo-sized pizza box.

I flap my tail up to 70 times a second to get enough power to launch out of the water.

I have five types of fins; the front four help me steer.

My long, narrow body is shaped like a submarine, and just like a submarine, I slide through water.

Who am I?

I AM A CALIFORNIA FLYING FISH

I move faster through air than I do through water—there's less resistance. My streamlined torpedo shape lets me gather the speed necessary to shoot into the air from the water. Then my extra-large front fins unfurl into wings, giving me the ability to glide just over the surface of the water.

When I start to lose height, I dip my tail into the water, flap wildly, and take off again. With a good wind I can glide for up to 600 feet—the length of about seven tennis courts.

I don't breathe during these leaps. I keep my gills closed so I don't lose too much moisture. Just like you leave the water to breathe air when swimming, I must return to the water to get my oxygen.

GUESS WHO ELSE IS

A SPECIAL FLYER

We are! We parachute from high places, using big pieces of nylon to slow our landing, much like the Malayan colugo. We take advantage of warming air currents to float up to the skies in a great hot air balloon, similar to the Rüppell's griffon vulture. We model the wings of tiny drones after the sword-billed hummingbird to explore hard-to-reach places. We build airplanes with long wings to travel great distances, just like the white-throated needletail.

We do all of this because although evolution will never give us the gift of flight, it has given us the gift of imagination and inspiration. We observe, admire, and invent based on the incredible flights of these record-breaking animals.

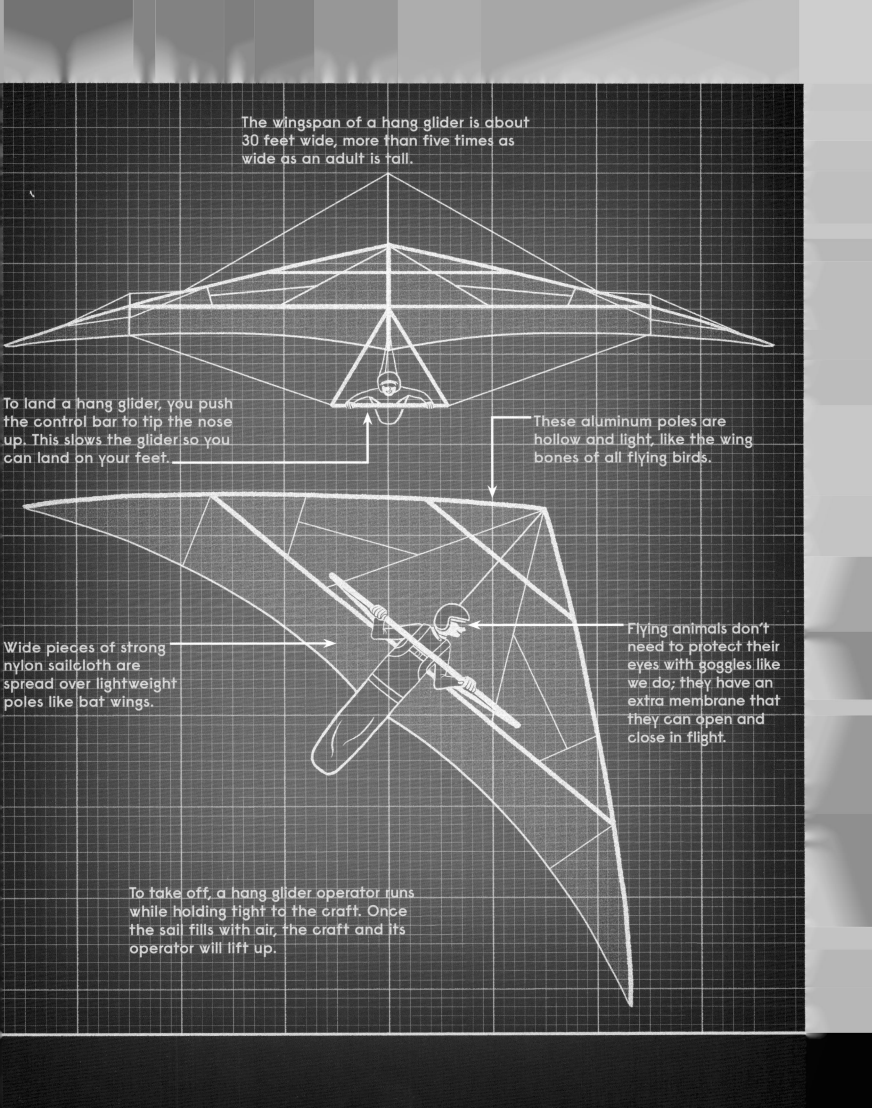

The wingspan of a hang glider is about 30 feet wide, more than five times as wide as an adult is tall.

To land a hang glider, you push the control bar to tip the nose up. This slows the glider so you can land on your feet.

These aluminum poles are hollow and light, like the wing bones of all flying birds.

Wide pieces of strong nylon sailcloth are spread over lightweight poles like bat wings.

Flying animals don't need to protect their eyes with goggles like we do; they have an extra membrane that they can open and close in flight.

To take off, a hang glider operator runs while holding tight to the craft. Once the sail fills with air, the craft and its operator will lift up.

Dear Reader,

I've always wished I could fly. So much so that the first rides I visit at the carnival are the ones that give you a sense of what it's like to soar through the air. On one of my favorite roller coasters two summers ago, I thought about how the dive of a peregrine falcon is a bit like the plummet of a coaster. I then wondered what other human activities had in common with animal flight. That curiosity led to this book.

The first step was choosing just ten animals from the millions of flyers around the world. I decided to pick one fish, one reptile, two insects, two mammals, and four birds. This let me examine different types of flight—flapping, soaring, gliding, and parachuting—across varying types of animals. Another writer might have chosen ten very different animals.

The next step was choosing how to measure each record. Take the fastest flyer. You can measure who flies the fastest while flapping, soaring, or diving. The answer is different for all three! As for the best at gliding, you could measure who travels the farthest, who glides most often, or who stays the most level while gliding. Again, the answer for each would reveal a different animal.

What about you? What animals and what record breakers would you have included? And what animal talent would inspire you to write a book? I hope you will share your discoveries and ideas with us when you decide!

Happy researching!
Gabe
Brooklyn, New York

FURTHER READING

At the library

Birds: Nature's Magnificent Flying Machines by Caroline Arnold and Patricia J. Wynne, Charlesbridge, 2003

A Butterfly is Patient by Dianna Hutts Aston and Sylvia Long, Chronicle, 2011

Natural History Museum: Book of Animal Records by Mark Carwardine, Firefly, 2013

Skulls: An Exploration of Alan Dudley's Curious Collection by Simon Winchester, Black Dog & Leventhal Publishers, Inc, 2012

On the Internet

American Museum of Natural History
www.amnh.org

The Cornell Lab of Ornithology
www.birdsleuth.org

Natural History Museum
www.nhm.ac.uk

Science Learning Hub
www.sciencelearn.org.nz

David Attenborough's Conquest of the Skies: First to Fly
www.smithsonianchannel.com

GLOSSARY OF FLIGHT WORDS

ow that you are a flight expert, use these words to talk like one too.

AERODYNAMIC (adjective): Aerodynamic objects move with great speed and efficiency. The shape of an aerodynamic object allows air to move past it with reduced drag. An airplane, torpedo, and white-throated needletail are aerodynamic. A bus, elephant, and house are not.

AIR CURRENT (noun): A large amount of air moving in the same direction. Birds like the Rüppell's griffon vulture lift from the ground using **thermals**, upward moving currents made by warm air.

DIVE (verb): A type of flight. To fall quickly at a steep angle. The Philippine eagle and other birds of prey dive to seize their prey quickly, and without warning.

DRAG (noun): Something that slows down the movement of something else. The Draco lizard spreads its **patagia** to create drag to slow its glide so it can land safely. Downhill skiers squeeze themselves into a tight crouch to make less drag and move faster. Airplanes open landing gear to create enough drag for a safe, slow landing.

EVOLUTION (noun): Small changes in the biology of plants, animals, and other living things over generations. Over thousands of years, evolutionary changes have given the flying animals in this book skills to survive and thrive.

FLAP (verb): To move one's arms or wings in a beating motion, usually up and down. Animals with smaller wings, like the hummingbird, flap more often than animals with larger wings, like the vulture.

FLY (verb): To move through air using wings. Flying is **powered movement**. This book looks at one fish, one reptile, two mammals, two insects, and four birds who all have some sort of wing.

GLIDE (verb): A type of flight. To move forward using air currents and without flapping wings. Gliding is **unpowered movement**. Large birds, bats, colugos, and flying squirrels are skilled gliders.

HOVER (verb): A type of flight. To hang in the air without moving forward or backward. Hovering is powered flight and uses a LOT of energy—just ask the dragonfly!

JET STREAM (noun): A long current of horizontal, high-speed winds that usually move faster than 250 miles per hour. Many birds with long wings take advantage of jet streams to soar long distances with little effort.

ORNITHOLOGIST (noun): A type of zoologist who studies some of the 18,000 species of birds on our planet.

PARACHUTE (verb): A type of flight. To fall using something, like cloth or skin, to create drag and slow your fall. Parachuting is **unpowered movement**. Colugos, the Draco lizard, and some snakes use flaps of skin, called **patagia**, to parachute. Once properly trained, humans can use nylon to parachute for sport or work.

PATAGIUM (noun) / PATAGIA (plural): The membrane or skin between the fore and hind limbs on a bat or gliding animal. Colugos, the Draco lizard, and some snakes have patagia. The patagium aids in gliding and parachuting flight.

POWERED MOVEMENT (noun): Using muscles—and not the wind or another outside force—to fly. The flapping flight of a dragonfly is powered movement.

SOAR (verb): A type of flight. Similar to gliding, an animal that soars uses air currents to move forward and upward. You must have a large wingspan to soar. Colugos, eagles, and vultures are excellent at soaring. Hummingbirds are not.

SPECIES (noun): A group of closely related plants, animals, and other living things that are similar to one another and can usually produce offspring. There are about 23 species of vulture, 170 species of megabat, and 550 species of swallowtail butterflies.

THERMAL (noun): A rising current of warm air. Hot air balloons and the Rüppell's griffon vulture use thermals to lift up in the air.

UNPOWERED MOVEMENT (noun): Staying in the air by using wind and air thermals instead of muscle effort. The soaring flight of the white-throated needletail is unpowered movement.

WING (noun): A part of an animal's body used for flying or gliding. A wing can be feathered, like a bird; scaled like a butterfly, dragonfly, and fish; or made of membrane, like the skin of a bat, colugo, and lizard.

WINGSPAN (noun): The distance between the tips of a pair of wings. The animal with the largest recorded wingspan was the now-extinct Chilean bony-toothed bird; it lived about five million years ago and had a wingspan of around 17 feet.